Daily English for College Students

Noriko Nakanishi Ai Hirai Mary Ellis

Book 1

SEIBIDO

photographs by
© iStockphoto
PIXTA

音声ファイルのダウンロード／ストリーミング

CD マーク表示がある箇所は、音声を弊社 HP より無料でダウンロード／ストリーミングすることができます。下記 URL の書籍詳細ページに音声ダウンロードアイコンがございますのでそちらから自習用音声としてご活用ください。

https://www.seibido.co.jp/708

**Daily English for College Students
Book 1**

Copyright © 2025 by Noriko Nakanishi, Ai Hirai,
Mary Ellis

*All rights reserved for Japan.
No part of this book may be reproduced in any form
without permission from Seibido Co., Ltd.*

はしがき

　翻訳ソフトやAIアプリのおかげで、日本語を入力すれば英語を簡単に表示させることができる時代になりました。しかし、その英文が場面に応じた自然な表現になっているかどうかはユーザ自身が判断する必要があります。同様に、英語を翻訳したときに表示される文字通りの日本語ではなく、その文が実際に何を目的としているかを理解していなければ思わぬ誤解を招くこともあります。さらに、音声を介した会話では、ほどよいテンポで、場面にふさわしい自分の言葉で相手とやり取りができるようになりたいものです。

　本書では、これまで英語を使用する経験があまりなかった大学生にも親しみやすいよう、大学の日常生活で起こりやすい話題を用意しました。日本の大学生マリとケンが、様々な国からの留学生と共に助け合いながら学生生活を送ります。「どんな場面で」「何のために」コミュニケーションを取るのかを意識すると、短い文で効率的にものごとを伝える表現を身につけることができます。本書は、これまで「英語を教わる」立場だったみなさんが、「英語を使う」人になれるよう、お手伝いをします。

　最後に、本書の出版にあたり、趣旨をご理解くださり、きめ細やかなアドバイスでサポートくださった(株)成美堂教材開発事業部の中澤ひろ子氏に、心から感謝を申し上げます。

2024年10月
筆者一同

本書の構成

各ユニットには、Listening セクションと Reading セクションがあります。

Listening

🎧 1 Warm-up for Listening

イラストを見ながら3つの短い文を聞き、T/F問題に解答します。
各ユニットのリスニングセクションで交わされる会話の場面設定を把握することが目的です。

🎧 2 Words and Phrases (1)

リスニングセクションに出てくるキーワードとそれに合致する意味を選ぶ問題です。少なくともこれらのキーワードは聞き取れるようになりましょう。

🎧 3 Listening Comprehension

2人の話者が、学生生活で起こりうる場面設定で会話をします。ページの余白を活かして、メモを取りながら聞く練習をしましょう。内容理解問題は5問あります。2人の会話の内容にふさわしい回答を選び、声に出して質問に答えましょう。

🎧 4 Dictation

前ページの Listening Comprehension の正答を導くヒントとなる語が空欄になっています。もう一度音声を聞いて単語を補充し、会話の内容理解を深めましょう。

🎧 5 Useful Expressions

各ユニットで取り上げる場面で役立つ表現を学習します。表現を応用して、自発的に発話できるようになりましょう。

［音声のポイント］

英語と日本語の音声の違いに注目します。英語らしいリズムやイントネーションを意識して聞き取り、発話するコツをつかみましょう。

Reading

📖 1 Warm-up for Reading

イラストを見ながら3つの短い文を聞き、T/F 問題に解答します。各ユニットの
リーディングセクションに関連する場面設定を把握することが目的です。

📖 2 Words and Phrases (2)

リーディングセクションに出てくるキーワードとそれに合致する意味を選ぶ問題で
す。リーディング問題に進む前に、これらのキーワードは理解しておきましょう。

📖 3 Reading

掲示物や web 情報、スライドのように、大学生活で頻繁に目にする文章から情報を
読み取る問題です。一文ずつ和訳するのではなく、その文章が何のために書かれて
いるかを理解して必要な情報を把握する練習をしましょう。

📖 4 Share Your Opinions

各ユニットの内容に関連したトピックが2問提示されます。ヒントを参考にしなが
ら自分の意見をまとめて書いたり話したりするだけでなく、クラスメイトの意見を
読んだり聞いたりして、要点をまとめる練習もしましょう。

📖 5 Grammar Practice

初歩的な文法事項を扱います。音声聞き取り問題を通して各ユニットで焦点が当て
られている文法事項を理解した上で、語句並べ替え問題によって、英作文の力を養
いましょう。

CONTENTS

Unit	Topic	Speakers	Useful Expressions
1	Nice to meet you. はじめまして	ケン（日本） ジェシー（アメリカ）	Greetings
2	I have an idea. 良い方法があるよ	マリ（日本） ルーカス（アメリカ）	Suggestions
3	There was a mistake in shipping. 発送ミスです！	ケン（日本） リリー（イギリス）	Complaints
4	I need a scholarship. 奨学金に挑戦！	マリ（日本） ジャック（イギリス）	Refusals
5	Vegetarian menu, please. 食堂へのお願い	ケン（日本） ルビー（オーストラリア）	Requests
6	Could you tell me more about it? 詳しい情報を教えて！	マリ（日本） デイブ（シンガポール）	Explanations
7	I've forgotten my password. パスワードを忘れた！	ケン（日本） アシャ（インド）	Apologies
8	I see what you mean. 気持ちはわかるよ	マリ（日本） イヴァン（ロシア）	Agreements
9	Good job! よくがんばったね	ケン（日本） ソフィア（ブラジル）	Compliments
10	Come and join us! 一緒にやってみない？	マリ（日本） エリック（中国）	Invitations
11	This will definitely help you. 就活必勝法	ケン（日本） サラ（エジプト）	Persuasion
12	Thanks for everything. 今までありがとう	マリ（日本） ジュリアス（ルワンダ）	Gratitude

	音声のポイント	Grammar Practice	Page
初回の授業に出席する場面で、クラスメイトに挨拶をする	英単語のアクセント	be 動詞	p.8
パソコンを買う場面で、提案をする	英語の母音	一般動詞	p.16
間違った商品が届いた場面で、苦情を伝える	英語の子音	助動詞	p.24
奨学金の申し込みをする場面で、依頼を断る	英語とカタカナ語	完了形	p.32
食堂のメニューについて、要望を伝える	英語のリズム	命令形	p.40
留学先について説明する	英語のイントネーション	受動態	p.48
パスワードを忘れて迷惑をかけた場面で、謝る	つながる音 (1)	前置詞・接続詞	p.56
友人が困ったことに遭遇している場面で、理解を示す	つながる音 (2)	形容詞	p.64
人の手助けをしようとする場面で、相手を励ます	聞こえなくなる音 (1)	副詞	p.72
ボランティア活動を始める場面で、友達を誘う	聞こえなくなる音 (2)	関係代名詞	p.80
履歴書の様式について、相手を説得する	まじりあう音 (1)	比較	p.88
お別れの場面で、感謝の気持ちを伝える	まじりあう音 (2)	仮定法	p.96

UNIT 1 Nice to meet you.

はじめまして。

🎧 LISTENING

Jessie and Ken are talking in the classroom.

🎧 1 | Warm-up for Listening

イラストを見ながら 1-3 の音声を聞き、内容が合っていれば T、合っていなければ F を選ぼう。

1　Two students are sitting by the door.　　　　　　　　　　T / F
2　They are talking with a professor.　　　　　　　　　　　 T / F
3　One of the students has a large bag.　　　　　　　　　　 T / F

🎧 2 | Words and Phrases (1)

1-5 の表現の意味に最も近いものを a-e から選ぼう。

1　professor　　　　　　　　　a　うわさ
2　seminar　　　　　　　　　　b　セミナー、ゼミ
3　exchange student　　　　　　c　教授
4　rumor　　　　　　　　　　　d　厳しい
5　strict　　　　　　　　　　　 e　留学生

UNIT 1　Nice to meet you.

🎧 3　Listening Comprehension   1-04~08

ジェシー（留学生）とケンの会話を聞いて、1-5の質問に対する正しい答えを選ぼう。

1　Where are Jessie and Ken?
　　❏ They are in Professor Smith's house.
　　❏ They are at the first year seminar class.

2　Is Jessie an exchange student?
　　❏ Yes, she is.
　　❏ No, she isn't.

3　Does Jessie want to sit next to Ken?
　　❏ Yes, she does.
　　❏ No, she doesn't.

4　Does Jessie know Professor Smith?
　　❏ Yes, she does.
　　❏ No, she doesn't.

5　How does Jessie feel now?
　　❏ She is nervous.
　　❏ She is not worried.

9

 **Dictation**

ジェシーとケンの会話をもう一度聞き、空欄を埋めよう。

1   Jessie: Excuse me. Is this Professor Smith's class?
    Ken: Yes. I think it's her _____ _____ _____.
    Jessie: Good. Thank you.

2   Ken: Are you an _____ _____ here?
    Jessie: _____, my name is Jessie.
    Ken: Nice to meet you, Jessie. I'm Ken.

3   Jessie: Nice to meet you too, Ken. Can I _____ _____ _____ _____?
    Ken: Sure. Let's sit over there.
    Jessie: OK. Do you know a lot about this university?

4   Ken: No, I just entered this university this year.
    Jessie: Me too. _____ _____ _____ anything about Professor Smith.
    Ken: I heard a rumor that she is strict about her class rules.

5   Jessie: I'm _____ _____.
    Ken: Don't worry. You will be OK.
    Jessie: Thanks. Oh, here comes the teacher.

UNIT 1 Nice to meet you.

🎧 5 | Useful Expressions: Greetings 1-09

ジェシーは "Excuse me." という表現を使って、ケンに声をかけました。こういった場面では、以下のような表現も役立ちます。どんなときに使える表現なのか考えて線でつなごう。

1　Excuse me. ●
2　Good morning. ●　　　　　　● 会話を始めるとき
3　Have a good day. ●
4　Hi. How are you? ●
5　See you soon. ●　　　　　　● 会話を終わらせるとき
6　Talk to you later. ●

音声のポイント　　**英単語のアクセント**　 1-10

単語の中で特定の部分が際立つように発音することを「アクセントを置く」といいます。日本語のアクセントは「セミナー」のように声の高低差で表現しますが、英語では "sem·i·nar" のように色付き文字の音節を高く強く長く発音して表現します。

以下の単語の発音を聞いて、色付き文字の音節が高く強く長く発音されていることを意識しながら、声に出して発音練習をしよう。

1　pro・**fes**・sor
2　**stu**・dent
3　u・ni・**ver**・si・ty
4　**ru**・mor
5　**nerv**・ous

11

READING

Classroom Rules
Be ready to learn.

Be on time.   Share your ideas.   Be nice to each other.

1 Warm-up for Reading 1-11

イラストを見ながら 1-3 の音声を聞き、内容が合っていれば T、合っていなければ F を選ぼう。

1　It tells you what you need to do in class.　　T / F

2　You shouldn't bring your watch to school.　　T / F

3　You should join in the discussion.　　T / F

2 Words and Phrases (2) 1-12

1-5 の表現の意味に最も近いものを a-e から選ぼう。

1　punctual　　　　　　a　貴重な、大切な

2　late submission　　　b　敬意を払う

3　precious　　　　　　c　時間（期限）を守る

4　respect　　　　　　 d　提出遅れ

5　atmosphere　　　　 e　雰囲気

UNIT 1　Nice to meet you.

 **Reading**　 1-13

以下のハンドアウトを読んで、1-3 の答えとして最もふさわしいものを選ぼう。

Professor Smith's class rules

Are you excited to join my class? The classroom is not a place just to have fun. Please remember the following rules.

✔ **Be punctual.**
I do not accept late submission of homework. Be in class on time. Don't waste the precious time you spend in the classroom.

✔ **Share your ideas.**
Do you want me to give you all the answers? I don't do that. Discussion is very important in this class. You need to find your own answer.

✔ **Respect each other.**
There is no completely correct answer. Respect each other's opinions. Create an atmosphere where everyone feels comfortable.

1　What does this handout show?
  A How to behave in Professor Smith's class.
  B How to hand in your homework.
  C How to get a correct answer from the teacher.
  D How to prove your answer is correct.

2　Which of the following is NOT mentioned?
  A Be on time.　　　　　B Respect the teacher.
  C Be active in class.　　D Value each other's opinion.

3　Which activity is most likely to be done in this class?
  A Essay writing.　　　　B Grammar exercises.
  C Listening practice.　　D Discussion.

4 Share Your Opinions 1-14,15

a Unit 1 では、初回の授業に出席する場面で、クラスメイトに声をかける表現を学びました。以下の質問に対するあなたの答えを、ヒントを参考にしながらまとめよう。

1 Are you good at starting conversations?
   Your answer:

   _____

   _____

> **Hint**
>
> - Yes. I…
>   enjoy talking with my friends.
>   can always find good topics.
>   like to make new friends.
>
> - No. I'm not good at it because…
>   I am shy.
>   I can't find a topic.
>   I wait for others to talk.

2 Talk to your classmates about class rules.
   Question: How do you start the conversation?
   Your answer:

   _____

   _____

> **Hint**
>
> - Excuse me. What do you think about _____ ?
> - Hi. How are you? Would you mind answering a few questions?
> - Good morning. Can I talk to you now?

b 上の質問に対するクラスメイトの答えを、以下の表にまとめよう。

Name	a 1	a 2

UNIT 1 Nice to meet you.

5 | Grammar Practice: be 動詞

 1-16, 17

英語の動詞にはbe動詞と一般動詞という2種類があります。ここではまずbe動詞について学びましょう。be動詞は「私は〜です。」のように主語が何であるかを説明する際に用いる動詞です。使われるbe動詞は、以下のように、主語と対応します。

主語	代名詞	現在（〜です）	過去（〜でした）
一人称 単数	I	am	was
二人称 単数	You	are	were
三人称 単数	He/She/It	is	was
一人称 複数	We	are	were
二人称 複数	You		
三人称 複数	They		

a 音声を聞き、以下の文の空欄を埋めよう。

1 She _____ strict about her class rules.

2 The classroom _____ _____ a place just to have fun.

3 _____ _____ Professor Smith's class?

b 音声を聞き、次の語句を並び替えて文を完成させよう。（文頭の文字は大文字に変えよう。）

1 英語の授業の宿題は簡単でした。
   [easy / English class / for / the homework / was].

2 私は留学生ではありません。
   [am / an / exchange student / I / not].

3 学生たちは常に時間を守っていましたか？
   [always / punctual / students / the / were]?

15

UNIT 2

I have an idea.
良い方法があるよ

🎧 LISTENING

Lucas and Mari are in a second-hand store.

🎧 1 Warm-up for Listening

イラストを見ながら 1-3 の音声を聞き、内容が合っていれば T、合っていなければ F を選ぼう。

1 There are only a few items in the store.　　　　　　　　T / F
2 Someone is standing in front of the counter.　　　　　　T / F
3 A student is showing the computer to the other student.　T / F

🎧 2 Words and Phrases (1)

1-5 の表現の意味に最も近いものを a-e から選ぼう。

1 second-hand　　　　　　a ノートパソコン
2 laptop　　　　　　　　　b 価格、値段
3 booklet　　　　　　　　 c 冊子
4 reasonable　　　　　　　d 手ごろな
5 price　　　　　　　　　 e 中古の

UNIT 2 I have an idea.

3 Listening Comprehension

 1-20~24

ルーカス（留学生）とマリの会話を聞いて、1-5 の質問に対する正しい答えを選ぼう。

1 Will Mari help Lucas?
   ❑ Yes, she will.
   ❑ No, she won't.

2 Does Lucas need everything on the list?
   ❑ Yes, he does.
   ❑ No, he doesn't.

3 Does Lucas have a computer?
   ❑ Yes, he does.
   ❑ No, he doesn't.

4 How does Lucas feel about buying a computer?
   ❑ He feels it's ok.
   ❑ He feels it's expensive.

5 What does Mari suggest?
   ❑ Checking for a second-hand laptop.
   ❑ Finding a reason to avoid buying a computer.

17

 **Dictation**

ルーカスとマリの会話をもう一度聞き、空欄を埋めよう。

1 Lucas: Hi Mari, I _____ a _____.
   Mari: Hi Lucas. What can I do for you?
   Lucas: I _____ _____ this booklet.

2 Mari: Oh, it shows a list of the things you need for your classes.
   Lucas: I know, but do I _____ _____ _____ _____?
   Mari: _____, you do. Why do you ask?

3 Lucas: Do I really have to buy a new computer?
   Mari: You _____ _____ _____?
   Lucas: _____. Can't I use my smartphone?

4 Mari: You can't do your homework without a computer.
   Lucas: Mm, but it's _____ _____.
   Mari: I have an idea, Lucas.

5 Lucas: What is it?
   Mari: Why don't you _____ ____ _____ - _____ _____?
   Lucas: OK. I hope they have one for a reasonable price.

UNIT 2　I have an idea.

5　Useful Expressions: Suggestions

マリは "Why don't you try a second-hand laptop?" という表現を使って、ルーカスにパソコン購入を勧めました。こういった場面では、以下のような表現も役立ちます。どんなときに使える表現なのか考えて線でつなごう。

1　How about…?　　　　　●
2　I'm not sure about that.　●　　　　　● 何かを勧めるとき
3　Let's….　　　　　　　●
4　Sounds like a good idea.　●
5　Why don't you…?　　　●　　　　　● 何かを勧められたとき
6　Sure. Why not?　　　　●

音声のポイント　　英語の母音　

日本語の母音は「アイウエオ」の5種類ですが、英語にはそれより多くの母音があります。例えばカタカナで示すと「ア」のように聞こえる音が、英語では別々の音として区別されることがあります。

以下の単語の発音を聞いて、色付き文字の母音の違いを意識しながら、声に出して発音練習をしよう。

1　a question　/ə kwéstʃən/
2　classes　/klǽsɪz | klάːsɪz/
3　one　/wʌ́n/
4　homework　/hóʊmwɚːrk/
5　laptop　/lǽptɑ̀p | lǽptɔ̀p/

READING

 Warm-up for Reading 1-27

イラストを見ながら 1-3 の音声を聞き、内容が合っていれば T、合っていなければ F を選ぼう。

1 It shows prices for desktop computers.　　　　　　　　T / F

2 All models are sold out.　　　　　　　　　　　　　　　T / F

3 There are some models that have discount prices.　　　T / F

 Words and Phrases (2) 1-28

1-5 の表現の意味に最も近いものを a-e から選ぼう。

1 school supplies　　　　　a 〜を消去する

2 in stock　　　　　　　　 b 学用品

3 payment　　　　　　　　c 在庫がある

4 refund　　　　　　　　　d 支払い

5 delete　　　　　　　　　 e 返金

UNIT 2　I have an idea.

 **Reading** 1-29

以下の web ページを読んで、1-3 の答えとして最もふさわしいものを選ぼう。

Laptops for Students

✔ Do you want to save money on school supplies?
✔ Do you want to get rid of your old laptop?

Why don't you come to the Student Center?
We help you buy and sell laptops.

> **Day:** Every Tuesday
> **Time:** 10:00-11:00 am
> **Location:** Student Center
> 　　　　　　(Building F, 1st floor)

When BUYING a laptop…	When SELLING your laptop…
· Click HERE to see the list of models in stock. · Come to the Student Center and tell us which one you want to buy. · Credit card payments only. · Sorry, no refunds.	· Delete all personal information on your laptop. · Click HERE and enter the information of your device. · Student Center staff will call you for more information.

1　Who is this information mainly for?
　　A　College students.　　B　Credit card company.
　　C　Bank employees.　　D　Computer developers.

2　Which of the following is NOT shown on this website?
　　A　Which day of the week they can help you.
　　B　Where to go when you need more information.
　　C　Which laptop you should buy.
　　D　What to do when you want to sell your laptop.

3　What do you need to do when buying a second-hand laptop?
　　A　Go to building F, 1st floor.　　B　Write your name on your PC.
　　C　Pay in cash.　　　　　　　　　D　Wait until they call you.

4 Share Your Opinions

 1-30, 31

a Unit 2 では、パソコンを買う場面で、提案をする表現を学びました。以下の質問に対するあなたの答えを、ヒントを参考にしながらまとめよう。

1 Do you like going to second-hand shops?
Your answer:

_____

_____

Hint

- Yes, because…
    prices are cheaper there.
    there are unique items.
    it's good for the environment.

- No. I prefer…
    brand new items.
    items with original tags.
    choosing from a variety of items.

2 Your friend is planning to buy a new computer.
Question: What do you suggest?
Your answer:

_____

_____

Hint

- Why don't you choose from your favorite brand?
- Let's compare the prices first.
- How about going to the store downtown together?

b 上の質問に対するクラスメイトの答えを、以下の表にまとめよう。

Name	**a** 1	**a** 2

22

UNIT 2　I have an idea.

5　Grammar Practice: 一般動詞

 1-32, 33

一般動詞は前回学習した be 動詞以外の全ての動詞です。Unit 1 で取り上げた be 動詞は主語に合わせて様々に変化しましたが、一般動詞では規則的に変化するもの（need、use など）、不規則に変化するもの（have、tell など）の 2 種類を覚えましょう。否定文、疑問文の語順にも注意しましょう。

原形	現在形 三人称単数	現在形 それ以外	過去形
need	needs	need	needed
use	uses	use	used
have	has	have	had
tell	tells	tell	told

a 音声を聞き、以下の文の空欄を埋めよう。

1　I _____ a question.

2　I _____ _____ this booklet.

3　____ you _____ to get rid of your old laptop?

b 音声を聞き、次の語句を並び替えて文を完成させよう。（文頭の文字は大文字に変えよう。）

1　ルーカスはお金を節約する必要があります。
　[Lucas / money / needs / save / to].

2　あなたはこのノートブックパソコンを買いたいですか。
　[buy / do / this laptop computer / want to / you]?

3　私の友達は私に値段を教えてくれなかった。
　[did / my friend / not / tell me / the price].

UNIT 3 — There was a mistake in shipping.

発送ミスです！

🎧 LISTENING

Lily and Ken are checking online orders.

🎧 1 Warm-up for Listening 1-34

イラストを見ながら 1-3 の音声を聞き、内容が合っていれば T、合っていなければ F を選ぼう。

1 There is a computer on the table. — T / F
2 Two students are looking at the computer screen. — T / F
3 The student in a white coat looks very happy. — T / F

🎧 2 Words and Phrases (1) 1-35

1-5 の表現の意味に最も近いものを a-e から選ぼう。

1 white coat (lab coat)   a 注文書、発注書
2 attach   b 〜を添付する
3 order form   c 白衣、診察着
4 shipping   d 発送、積み込み、送料
5 complaint   e 不満、苦情

UNIT 3　There was a mistake in shipping.

🎧 3　Listening Comprehension

リリー（留学生）とケンの会話を聞いて、1-5 の質問に対する正しい答えを選ぼう。

1　Is the white coat Ken's?
　❑ Yes, it is.
　❑ No, it isn't.

2　What size did Lily order?
　❑ Extra-small.
　❑ Extra-large.

3　Is Lily surprised that there was a mistake?
　❑ Yes, she is.
　❑ No, she isn't.

4　What does Ken suggest?
　❑ Order a new coat.
　❑ Write an email.

5　Will Lily attach a photo to the email?
　❑ Yes, she will.
　❑ No, she won't.

 **Dictation** 1-36~40

リリーとケンの会話をもう一度聞き、空欄を埋めよう。

1 Lily: Can you look at this white coat, Ken?
   Ken: Wow! That's very big! _____ _____ _____?
   Lily: _____. I'm sure I ordered an extra-small coat.

2 Ken: Do you have the order form?
   Lily: Here. _____ _____ a _____ _____ on _____-_____.
   Ken: There must be a mistake in shipping.

3 Lily: I can't believe it.
   Ken: It sometimes happens.
   Lily: I _____ it _____ _____ _____ in _____!

4 Ken: Of course, it happens everywhere.
   Lily: You're right. Should I make a complaint?
   Ken: Sure. _____ _____ _____ and attach the _____ _____.

5 Lily: Good idea. I'll _____ _____ a _____ of the coat.
   Ken: Then, they will know it's their mistake.
   Lily: Right. I have to hurry now.

UNIT 3　There was a mistake in shipping.

 5 | **Useful Expressions: Complaints** 1-41

リリーは "Should I make a complaint?" という表現を使って、業者にクレームを送るべきかケンに相談しました。こういった場面では、以下のような表現も役立ちます。どんなときに使える表現なのか考えて線でつなごう。

1　Excuse me, but there is a problem.　●

2　I will look into this right away.　●　　●苦情を伝えるとき

3　I'll deal with it immediately.　●

4　I'm sorry, but there's nothing I can do.　●

5　It's probably not your fault, but….　●　　●苦情を伝えられたとき

6　Excuse me, something is wrong with….　●

音声のポイント　　**英語の子音**　 1-42

「カキクケコ」をローマ字で表記すると「ka ki ku ke ko」となるように、日本語の子音の後にはたいてい母音が続きますが、英語では子音で終わる語が多くありますし、子音が2つ以上連続することも頻繁にあります。

以下の単語の発音を聞いて、色付き文字の子音の後に母音が続かないこと、または子音が連続していることを意識しながら、声に出して発音練習をしよう。

1　coat　/kóʊt/
2　big　/bíg/
3　extra　/ékstrə/
4　mistake　/mɪstéɪk/
5　complaint　/kəmpléɪnt/

READING

Your Order

White Coat (Lab Coat)
☑ XS ☐ S ☐ M ☐ L ☐ XL
¥2,590
Condition: New
Shipping within 24 hours

1 Warm-up for Reading 1-43

イラストを見ながら 1-3 の音声を聞き、内容が合っていれば T、合っていなければ F を選ぼう。

1 This form shows the order information.　　T / F

2 There is no information about the size of the coat.　　T / F

3 The coat will be shipped within a day.　　T / F

2 Words and Phrases (2) 1-44

1-5 の表現の意味に最も近いものを a-e から選ぼう。

1 condition　　　　　　　a 〜することになっている

2 customer　　　　　　　b 顧客、取引先

3 detail　　　　　　　　c 詳細、細部

4 product　　　　　　　d 状態、状況、条件

5 be supposed to…　　　e 製品、商品

UNIT 3　There was a mistake in shipping.

 Reading 1-45

以下の入力フォームを読んで、1-3 の答えとして最もふさわしいものを選ぼう。

Customer Complaint Form

First Name	Last Name	
Lily	Jones	
Email Address	**Email Address (Type again.)**	**Phone Number**
l_jones@ch.daily.ac.jp	l_jones@ch.daily.ac.jp	+81-78-123-4567
Product	**Reason for Complaint**	**Date of Order**
☑ White Coat (Lab Coat)	☑ delivery ☑ wrong size	Apr. 27, 2025

Details of Complaint

I ordered a white coat through your website two weeks ago, and it was delivered today. According to your website, shipping was supposed to be within 24 hours.

Also, I ordered a size XS but received an XL instead.

I need this lab coat for my class next week. Could you please send me a size XS as soon as possible? Please let me know when it is shipped.

Thank you.

1　This form is for the customers to _____ .
　A apologize　B complain　C advertize　D order

2　When did Lily order the coat?
　A In March.　B In April.　C In May.　D In June.

3　What does Lily need for her class?
　A An email.　B A webpage.　C A receipt.　D A lab coat.

4 Share Your Opinions

 2-46, 47

a Unit 3 では、間違った商品が届いた場面で、苦情を伝える表現を学びました。以下の質問に対するあなたの答えを、ヒントを参考にしながらまとめよう。

1 Do you like buying your clothes online?
Your answer:

___

___

Hint

- Yes, I like online shopping because…
    it's more convenient.
    I don't want to talk with the staff.
    too many people are in the stores.

- No, real stores are better because…
    I can get my friends' opinions.
    I can try them on.
    the colors look different online.

2 You don't like the item you bought at a store.
Question: How do you complain to the store staff?
Your answer:

___

___

Hint

- Excuse me, something is wrong with this item. Can I return it, please?
- Excuse me, but there is a problem with this item I bought.
- It's probably not your fault, but I'm not satisfied with this item.

b 上の質問に対するクラスメイトの答えを、以下の表にまとめよう。

Name	a 1	a 2

UNIT 3　There was a mistake in shipping.

5 | Grammar Practice: 助動詞

 1-48, 49

助動詞は動詞に新たなニュアンスを追加する機能を持ちます。例えば I study English.（私は英語を勉強する）という文で動詞 (study) の前に should や will を置くと「私は英語を勉強すべきである」や「私は英語を勉強するつもりである」という意味になります。

助動詞	意味	例
can	できる	You can do it for sure.
	になりうる	It can be dangerous.
should	すべきである	He should go to see the doctor.
may	かもしれない	The teachers may be right.
will	だろう	The train will leave soon.

a 音声を聞き、以下の文の空欄を埋めよう。

1　There _____ _____ a mistake in shipping.

2　I _____ _____ it.

3　_____ _____ please send me a size XS?

b 音声を聞き、次の語句を並び替えて文を完成させよう。（文頭の文字は大文字に変えよう。）

1　あなたはメールを書くべきです。
[an / email / should / write / you].

2　細部をお見せすることができます。
[can / I / show / the details / you].

3　来週木曜までに送ってもらえますか？
[by / could / next Thursday / send it / you]?

31

UNIT 4 I need a scholarship.

奨学金に挑戦！

🎧 LISTENING

Professors are looking at documents and having a discussion.

🎧 1　Warm-up for Listening

イラストを見ながら 1-3 の音声を聞き、内容が合っていれば T、合っていなければ F を選ぼう。

1　They are walking around the table.　　　　　　　　　　T / F
2　They are holding documents.　　　　　　　　　　　　　T / F
3　No one is interested in the discussion.　　　　　　　　T / F

🎧 2　Words and Phrases (1)

1-5 の表現の意味に最も近いものを a-e から選ぼう。

1　scholarship　　　　　　　a　〜に申し込む、応募する
2　rewrite　　　　　　　　　b　〜を書き直す
3　apply for　　　　　　　　c　却下する、拒否する
4　submit　　　　　　　　　d　奨学金
5　reject　　　　　　　　　　e　提出する

UNIT 4　I need a scholarship.

🎧 3　Listening Comprehension　 1-52~56

ジャック（留学生）とマリの会話を聞いて、1-5 の質問に対する正しい答えを選ぼう。

1　Has Jack applied for a scholarship before?
   ❏ Yes, he has.
   ❏ No, he hasn't.

2　How does Jack feel about the rejection?
   ❏ He feels happy.
   ❏ He feels sorry.

3　Who needs help in rewriting the form?
   ❏ Jack does.
   ❏ Mari does.

4　Will Jack rewrite the application for Mari?
   ❏ Yes, he will.
   ❏ No, he won't.

5　Will Mari see Jack tonight?
   ❏ Yes, she will.
   ❏ No, she won't.

33

 **Dictation**

ジャックとマリの会話をもう一度聞き、空欄を埋めよう。

1 Mari: Jack, have you ever _____ __ __ _____?
   Jack: _____. How can I help you, Mari?
   Mari: I want to apply for the study-abroad scholarship.

2 Jack: I thought you had already submitted the application.
   Mari: Yes, but they have rejected it.
   Jack: Oh, I'm _____ __ _____ __.

3 Mari: But they have given me a second chance.
   Jack: I see. Do you need _____ _____ in _____ the _____?
   Mari: _____, please. Do you have some time now?

4 Jack: Sorry, I have a class in five minutes. How about tomorrow?
   Mari: Great. Can you rewrite the application for me?
   Jack: I'm _____ I _____ _____ __ _____, Mari.

5 Mari: I understand. I'll rewrite it myself tonight.
   Jack: Sure, then I'd be happy to give you some advice.
   Mari: Thanks! _____ _____ _____.

UNIT 4　I need a scholarship.

🎧 5　Useful Expressions: Refusals

ジャックは "I'm afraid I shouldn't do that." という表現を使って、マリからの依頼を断りました。こういった場面では、以下のような表現も役立ちます。どんなときに使える表現なのか考えて線でつなごう。

1　Certainly not.　　　●
2　I wish I could, but….　●　　　　　　● ていねいに断るとき
3　I'm afraid I can't….　●
4　I'm sorry, but….　　●
5　No way.　　　　　　●　　　　　　● 断固として断るとき
6　That's not possible.　●

音声のポイント　　英語とカタカナ語

カタカナ語としてなじみがある語でも、英単語とは拍の取り方が大きく異なることがあります。例えば日本語で「ヘルプ」は3拍で発音されますが、英語の help には母音が1つしかないため、1音節の語と見なされます。

以下の単語の発音を聞いて、それぞれの単語がいくつの音節で成り立っているかを意識しながら、声に出して発音練習をしよう。

1　chance　/tʃæns | tʃɑːns/
2　please　/pliːz/
3　ad•vice　/ədváɪs/
4　schol•ar•ship　/skɑ́lərʃɪp | skɔ́ləʃɪp/
5　ap•pli•ca•tion　/ӕplɪkéɪʃən/

READING

XYZ University Study-Abroad Scholarship Programs

	Full scholarship	Partial scholarship
Air tickets	✓	✗
School fees	✓	✓
Homestay	✓	✗
Health insurance	✓	✗

1 Warm-up for Reading

イラストを見ながら 1-3 の音声を聞き、内容が合っていれば T、合っていなければ F を選ぼう。

1　The chart shows the types of scholarships.　　T / F

2　Both scholarships help you with the cost of education.　　T / F

3　Homestay costs are covered in the partial scholarship.　　T / F

2 Words and Phrases (2)

1-5 の表現の意味に最も近いものを a-e から選ぼう。

1	partial	a	（人）に〜を推薦する
2	review	b	検閲する、見直す
3	unfortunately	c	残念ながら
4	recommend	d	部分的な
5	resume	e	履歴書

UNIT 4   I need a scholarship.

 **Reading**

以下のメールを読んで、1-3の答えとして最もふさわしいものを選ぼう。

Dear Mari Sato,

   Thank you for applying to the full scholarship program. We received many applications this year. It was hard to choose just one person. We carefully reviewed your application. Unfortunately, you have not made it this time.

   However, you have a second chance. You can now apply for partial scholarships. Please see the attached file which gives details.

   We recommend you update your resume. Please send your new resume with the application. This will help us understand you better.

   We look forward to receiving your updated application.

Best regards,
Grace Murphy

---

1 Who was this email sent to?
   A To Grace Murphy.   B To the president.
   C To XYZ University.   D To Mari Sato.

2 Mari had applied for the _____ program.
   A fully funded scholarship   B study-abroad
   C partial funding scholarship D XYZ University internship

3 What does Mari need to do to apply for the scholarship again?
   A Receive more applications.   B Select the candidates.
   C Recommend a new program.   D Send a new application form.

4 Share Your Opinions

 1-62, 63

a Unit 4 では、奨学金の申し込みをする場面で、依頼を断る表現を学びました。以下の質問に対するあなたの答えを、ヒントを参考にしながらまとめよう。

1 Have you ever applied for a scholarship?
   Your answer:

   _____

   _____

> **Hint**
>
> - Yes, I've applied…
>   for an overseas scholarship program.
>   for the one from the government.
>   because my teacher selected me.
>
> - No, I haven't, …
>   but I'm thinking about it.
>   because I had no chance.
>   because I don't need one.

2 Your friend is asking you to do homework for her/him.
   Question: How do you refuse this request?
   Your answer:

   _____

   _____

> **Hint**
>
> - I'm sorry, but I think you should do it yourself.
> - I'm afraid I can't, because I haven't done mine yet.
> - I wish I could, but I don't have time now.

b 上の質問に対するクラスメイトの答えを、以下の表にまとめよう。

Name	**a** 1	**a** 2

UNIT 4　I need a scholarship.

5　Grammar Practice: 完了形

 1-64, 65

完了形とは、過去から現在までの間に何が起こっていたかを説明する形です。I have lost my key. のように、have に動詞の過去分詞形が続きます。過去形の I lost my key. では、過去に鍵をなくしたけれど見つかったのか今もないのか不明ですが、完了形の I have lost my key. では鍵は過去になくなりそして今もない、ということがわかります。

完了形の例	意味
I have known her for three years.	私は彼女と 3 年来の知り合いです。
Has he lived there for two years?	彼はそこに 2 年住んでいますか？
I have not finished my homework.	まだ宿題が終わっていません。
Jessie has never driven a car.	Jessie は運転したことがありません。

a 音声を聞き、以下の文の空欄を埋めよう。

1　You _____ already _____ the application.

2　You _____ _____ _____ it.

3　_____ _____ ever _____ for a scholarship?

b 音声を聞き、次の語句を並び替えて文を完成させよう。（文頭の文字は大文字に変えよう。）

1　私は奨学金に応募しました。
　[applied / for / have / I / the scholarship].

　_____

2　彼はその書類をまだ提出していません。
　[has not / he / submitted / the document / yet].

　_____

3　台湾に行ったことがありますか？
　[been / ever / have / to Taiwan / you]?

　_____

39

UNIT 5 Vegetarian menu, please.

食堂へのお願い

🎧 LISTENING

There are lots of people in the university cafeteria.

🎧 1 Warm-up for Listening 1-66

イラストを見ながら 1-3 の音声を聞き、内容が合っていれば T、合っていなければ F を選ぼう。

1	The cafeteria is closed.	T / F
2	There is no one in front of the ticket machine.	T / F
3	Pictures of some dishes are displayed.	T / F

🎧 2 Words and Phrases (1) 1-67

1-5 の表現の意味に最も近いものを a-e から選ぼう。

1	vegetarian	a	アレルギー
2	meat	b	ベジタリアン
3	allergy	c	苦しむ、耐える
4	suffer	d	掲示板
5	message board	e	食肉

UNIT 5　Vegetarian menu, please.

🎧 3 Listening Comprehension   1-68~72

ルビー（留学生）とケンの会話を聞いて、1-5 の質問に対する正しい答えを選ぼう。

1　Does Ken want to go to the new cafeteria?
　❏ Yes, he does.
　❏ No, he doesn't.

2　What is Ruby worried about?
　❏ She forgot her lunch today.
　❏ She can't eat meat.

3　Will Ruby talk to the cafeteria staff in Japanese?
　❏ Yes, she will.
　❏ No, she won't.

4　Who has a food allergy?
　❏ Ruby does.
　❏ Ken's friend does.

5　Is Ruby thinking about making a request to the cafeteria?
　❏ Yes, she is.
　❏ No, she isn't.

 **Dictation**

ルビーとケンの会話をもう一度聞き、空欄を埋めよう。

1. Ken: Hi, Ruby. _____ ____ to the _____ _____ for lunch.
   Ruby: OK, but I hope there is something I can eat.
   Ken: What do you mean?

2. Ruby: You know _____ _____ _____ _____, right?
   Ken: Oh, that's right. I totally forgot about it.
   Ruby: Do they have a vegetarian menu?

3. Ken: I don't know. Just ask them which dish has no meat.
   Ruby: Can you help me if they don't _____ my _____?
   Ken: Sure. But try your best, and let me know when you need help.

4. Ruby: Thanks, Ken.
   Ken: Come to think of it, my _____ suffers from a shrimp allergy.
   Ruby: Shrimp? It's everywhere!

5. Ken: Right. He also needs the vegetarian menu.
   Ruby: Now, _____ _____ ____ _____ a _____?
   Ken: Well, there is a message board in the cafeteria.

UNIT 5 Vegetarian menu, please.

🎧 5 Useful Expressions: Requests 1-73

ルビーは "Can you help me if they don't understand my Japanese?" という表現を使って、ケンに手助けを依頼しました。こういった場面では、以下のような表現も役立ちます。どんなときに使える表現なのか考えて線でつなごう。

1 Certainly. ●
2 Could you please…? ●   ● 依頼をするとき
3 Do you mind…? ●
4 I'd be happy to…. ●
5 I'm sorry, but I can't. ●   ● 依頼を受けたとき
6 Would it be possible for you to…? ●

音声のポイント　　英語のリズム 1-74

「一緒に**ランチ**に**行こう**」と言うとき、太字の語と小さい「に」の音の強さは異なるはずです。このように、日本語でも英語でも、文の中で重要な意味を持つ語（内容語）はハッキリと強く長く、文法上の働きを持つ語（機能語）は弱く短く発音されます。

以下の文の発音を聞いて、色付きの部分が強く長く、それ以外の小さい文字は弱く短く発音されていることを意識しながら、声に出して発音練習をしよう。

1　**What** do you **mean**?
2　Do they **have** a vege**tar**ian **men**u?
3　**Let** me **know** when you **need help**.
4　My **friend suf**fers from a **shrimp al**lergy.
5　**How** shall we **make** a re**quest**?

READING

GRAND OPENING

Opening hours: Mon－Fri 10:00－17:00

Welcome to DAILY CAFE

Leave a note for the kitchen staff on the communication board. We welcome your opinions.

1 Warm-up for Reading

イラストを見ながら 1-3 の音声を聞き、内容が合っていれば T、合っていなければ F を選ぼう。

1 This is a menu of Daily Cafe.   T / F
2 You can enjoy lunch at this cafe on Saturdays.   T / F
3 They want to hear your opinions.   T / F

2 Words and Phrases (2)

1-5 の表現の意味に最も近いものを a-e から選ぼう。

1 crowded   a ～を陣取る、占有する
2 essential   b 混雑した
3 religious beliefs c 宗教的信念
4 occupy   d 絶対必要な
5 boxed lunch   e 弁当

UNIT 5 Vegetarian menu, please.

📖 3 Reading

以下の掲示板のメッセージを読んで、1-3の答えとして最もふさわしいものを選ぼう。

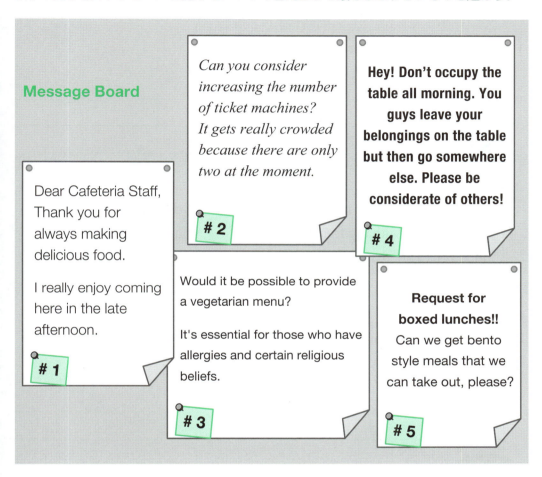

1. How many ticket machines does this cafeteria have now?
   A One.   B Two.   C Three.   D Four.

2. The message _____ is a request to the students, not to the cafeteria staff.
   A #2   B #3   C #4   D #5

3. If you want to enjoy a meal outdoors, you would agree to message _____ .
   A #1   B #2   C #3   D #5

4 Share Your Opinions 1-78, 79

a Unit 5 では、食堂のメニューについて、要望を伝える表現を学びました。以下の質問に対するあなたの答えを、ヒントを参考にしながらまとめよう。

1 Do you often go to the school cafeteria?
   Your answer:

   _____

   _____

   Hint
   - Yes,…
       it's easier than making my own lunch.
       I enjoy lunch with my friends.
       their prices are reasonable.
   - No,….
       I bring my own lunch.
       I buy packed meals.
       I don't have time to go there.

2 You want to improve your English writing skills.
   Question: How do you ask your teacher for help?
   Your answer:

   _____

   _____

   Hint
   - Could you please check my writing?
   - Do you mind giving me some assistance in correcting my English?
   - Would it be possible for you to help me?

b 上の質問に対するクラスメイトの答えを、以下の表にまとめよう。

Name	a 1	a 2

UNIT 5   Vegetarian menu, please.

5 Grammar Practice: 命令形   1-80, 81

命令形とは、相手に命令、依頼、提案、勧誘などをする際に用いる文の形です。Wash your hands. のように主語は省略されます。命令文を少し弱めるには文頭や文末に please をつけます。命令形は友達以外にはあまり使用しませんが、道案内のような指示文では基本的に命令形で説明し、また please を付けることもありません。

意図	例	意味
命令	Watch your step.	足元に気を付けて。
指示	Turn left at the next corner.	次の角を左に曲がってください。
依頼	Send me the document, please.	書類を送付してください。
提案	Let me handle this.	私に任せて。
勧誘	Let's go to the movie.	映画を観に行きましょう。

a 音声を聞き、以下の文の空欄を埋めよう。

1 _____ ____ ____ the new cafeteria for lunch.

2 Just _____ them which dish has no meat.

3 _____ _____ the table all morning.

b 音声を聞き、次の語句を並び替えて文を完成させよう。（文頭の文字は大文字に変えよう。）

1 まっすぐ行って次の角を左に曲がってください。
[and / at the next corner / go / straight / turn left].

2 カフェのスタッフと話をしましょう。
[cafe staff / let's / talk / the / with].

3 ミスは気にしないでね。
[about / don't / mistake / worry / your].

UNIT 6 Could you tell me more about it?

詳しい情報を教えて！

🎧 LISTENING

Mari is giving a presentation in the classroom.

🎧 1 Warm-up for Listening

イラストを見ながら 1-3 の音声を聞き、内容が合っていれば T、合っていなければ F を選ぼう。

1 There is a screen in front of the classroom.　　T / F
2 A student is explaining something to other students.　　T / F
3 All of the students are chatting with each other.　　T / F

🎧 2 Words and Phrases (1)

1-5 の表現の意味に最も近いものを a-e から選ぼう。

1 explain   a 〜を提供する
2 chat   b しゃべる、チャットする
3 overseas field trip c すばらしい
4 awesome   d 海外研修、海外調査旅行
5 serve   e 説明する、弁明する

UNIT 6　Could you tell me more about it?

🎧 3 Listening Comprehension

デイブ（留学生）とマリの会話を聞いて、1-5 の質問に対する正しい答えを選ぼう。

1　Is Dave joining the field trip?
　❏ Yes, he is.
　❏ No, he isn't.

2　Where is Dave from?
　❏ He is from Singapore.
　❏ He is from China.

3　Is Mari interested in the Night Safari?
　❏ Yes, she is.
　❏ No, she isn't.

4　Are there many Chinese people in Singapore?
　❏ Yes, there are.
　❏ No, there aren't.

5　What is Mari interested in?
　❏ She is interested in English accents in Singapore.
　❏ She is interested in what Dave likes to do in Singapore.

 **Dictation**

デイブとマリの会話をもう一度聞き、空欄を埋めよう。

1 Dave: What are you going to do during the summer vacation?
   Mari: I'll _____ the _____ _____ _____.
   Dave: Sounds good, but where are you going?

2 Mari: I'm going to _____ _____, _____.
   Dave: That's awesome. How long are you going to be there?
   Mari: I'll be there for two weeks. Any place you recommend?

3 Dave: Why don't you visit the _____ _____?
   Mari: Safari at night! I _____ to _____ _____. Anything else?
   Dave: Chinese food is also good.

4 Mari: Why is Chinese food served in Singapore?
   Dave: Because _____ _____ _____ _____ _____.
   Mari: Is English spoken by Chinese people?

5 Dave: Yes. English is _____ with _____.
   Mari: Interesting. Could you tell me more about it?
   Dave: Of course. Ask me anything you like.

UNIT 6　Could you tell me more about it?

🎧 5　Useful Expressions: Explanations 1-89

デイブは "Where are you going?"、"How long are you going to be there?" などの表現を使って、マリが説明しやすいように質問しました。こういった場面では、以下のような表現も役立ちます。どんなときに使える表現なのか考えて線でつなごう。

1　Could you explain that again?　●
2　Do you want the details?　●　　　　● 説明したいとき
3　I mean, ….　●
4　Let me explain.　●
5　What do you mean?　●　　　　● 説明してほしいとき
6　Will you tell me about…?　●

音声のポイント　　英語のイントネーション　 1-90

ことばを話すときの、声の上がり下がりによっておこる音の高さの変化はイントネーションと呼ばれます。基本的に、yes-no 疑問文は上がり調子、wh 疑問文・否定文・肯定文は下がり調子で話されますが、そうでない場合も多くあります。

以下の文の発音を聞いて、文末が上がり調子（↗）、下がり調子（↘）になっていることを意識しながら、声に出して発音練習をしよう。

1　Where are you going?　（↘）
2　Any place you recommend?　（↗）
3　Chinese food is also good.　（↘）
4　Many Chinese people live there.　（↘）
5　Could you tell me more about it?　（↗）

51

READING

Overseas Field Trip Schedule

Day 1	Arrival (Changi Airport)	*Day 3: Prepare presentation slides about Singapore BEFORE joining the program.
Day 2	Welcome party **(optional)** Night Safari tour	
Day 3	1ˢᵗ presentation *	

1 Warm-up for Reading

イラストを見ながら 1-3 の音声を聞き、内容が合っていれば T、合っていなければ F を選ぼう。

1 This chart shows the schedule for a field trip. T / F

2 Everyone must join the Night Safari tour. T / F

3 You need to make presentation slides before the program. T / F

2 Words and Phrases (2)

1-5 の表現の意味に最も近いものを a-e から選ぼう。

1 ethnic group   a ～に影響を及ぼす

2 official language   b 公用語

3 frequently   c 正式ではない

4 informal   d 頻繁に

5 influence   e 民族

52

UNIT 6　Could you tell me more about it?

3　Reading

 1-93

以下の発表スライドを読んで、1-3 の答えとして最もふさわしいものを選ぼう。

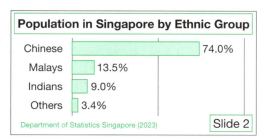

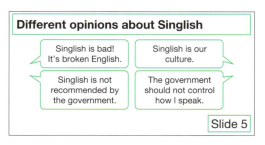

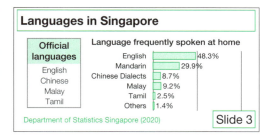

1　The majority of the population in Singapore is _____ .
　A　Chinese　　　B　Malay　　　C　Indian　　　D　others

2　How many official languages are there in Singapore?
　A　One.　　　B　Two.　　　C　Three.　　　D　Four.

3　Which slide shows opinions about using Singlish?
　A　Slide 2.　　　B　Slide 3.　　　C　Slide 4.　　　D　Slide 5.

4 Share Your Opinions 1-94, 95

a Unit 6 では、留学先について説明する表現を学びました。以下の質問に対するあなたの答えを、ヒントを参考にしながらまとめよう。

1 Do you want to visit foreign countries?
   Your answer:

   _____

   _____

   Hint
   - Yes, because I want to…
     experience something new.
     practice speaking in a foreign language.
     meet people from different cultures.
   - No,….
     I like staying in Japan.
     I'm afraid to visit new places.
     I don't have enough money.

2 Your friends want to know how to get to your favorite place.
   Question: How do you explain it?
   Your answer:

   _____

   _____

   Hint
   - My favorite place is _____. Let me explain how to get there.
   - I like going to _____. I mean, _____ is the best.
   - There's _____ in my neighborhood. Do you want the details?

b 上の質問に対するクラスメイトの答えを、以下の表にまとめよう。

Name	a 1	a 2

UNIT 6 Could you tell me more about it?

5 Grammar Practice: 受動態 1-96, 97

「誰かが何かを〇〇する」という形は能動態ですが、一方「何かが誰かに〇〇される」という受け身の形を受動態と呼びます。英語では、be 動詞と動詞の過去分詞形を用いて受動態を表現します。

能動態	受動態
The staff cleans the rooms.	The rooms are cleaned by the staff.
My grandfather named me.	I was named by my grandfather.
He did not send the letter.	The letter was not sent by him.
Does a king rule your country?	Is your country ruled by a king?
Did she write this story?	Was this story written by her?

a 音声を聞き、以下の文の空欄を埋めよう。

1. It _____ _____ by other languages.

2. Singlish _____ _____ _____ by the government.

3. _____ English _____ by Chinese people?

b 音声を聞き、次の語句を並び替えて文を完成させよう。（文頭の文字は大文字に変えよう。）

1. 若者に好まれるレストランがあります。
   [are / by / preferred / some restaurants / young people].

2. タミル語はインドで話されますか？
   [in / India / is / spoken / Tamil]?

3. ここではアメリカ式の綴りは使用されません。
   [here / is / not / the American spelling system / used].

UNIT 7 I've forgotten my password.

パスワードを忘れた！

🎧 LISTENING

Asha and Ken are talking in the International Student Center.

🎧 1 Warm-up for Listening

 2-02

イラストを見ながら 1-3 の音声を聞き、内容が合っていれば T、合っていなければ F を選ぼう。

1	Both students are seated.	T / F
2	There is no table in the room.	T / F
3	One of them seems to be sorry about something.	T / F

🎧 2 Words and Phrases (1)

 2-03

1-5 の表現の意味に最も近いものを a-e から選ぼう。

1	translate		a	～に感謝する
2	bother		b	～の邪魔をする、～を悩ます
3	stupid		c	～を翻訳する
4	available		d	馬鹿げた、頭の悪い
5	appreciate		e	利用できる、空いている

UNIT 7   I've forgotten my password.

🎧 3 | Listening Comprehension

アシャ（留学生）とケンの会話を聞いて、1-5の質問に対する正しい答えを選ぼう。

1 Does Ken want help from Asha?
   ❏ Yes, he does.
   ❏ No, he doesn't.

2 What is the problem with Asha?
   ❏ She can't enter her username.
   ❏ She has forgotten her password.

3 Did Asha check the website by herself?
   ❏ Yes, she did.
   ❏ No, she didn't.

4 Is the form written in Japanese?
   ❏ Yes, it is.
   ❏ No, it isn't.

5 What will Ken do next?
   ❏ He will translate the form into English.
   ❏ He will translate the form into Japanese.

 **Dictation**

アシャとケンの会話をもう一度聞き、空欄を埋めよう。

1 Asha: Hi, Ken. Sorry to bother you, but _____ _____ _____ _____?
   Ken: _____ _____. What happened?
   Asha: I cannot log into the university system.

2 Ken: Enter your username and password here.
   Asha: I can't do that because I've _____ my _____.
   Ken: Oh, then let me check the ICT website for you.

3 Asha: How stupid of me! I _____ _____ _____ it by myself.
   Ken: Don't worry. It says you type in your information here.
   Asha: Thank you, Ken.

4 Ken: Here you are. Can you fill it in, please?
   Asha: Uh, don't they have an _____ _____?
   Ken: I'm _____ they _____ _____ it available in English.

5 Asha: Oh, too bad.
   Ken: I can _____ it into _____ for you.
   Asha: Thanks, and I appreciate your help.

UNIT 7 I've forgotten my password.

🎧 5 Useful Expressions: Apologies

アシャは "Sorry to bother you." という表現を使って、ケンの邪魔をするかもしれないことに対して謝ってから話し始めました。こういった場面では、以下のような表現も役立ちます。どんなときに使える表現なのか考えて線でつなごう。

1　Apology accepted.　●
2　Don't worry.　●　　　　　　●　謝るとき
3　I'm sorry….　●
4　It's my fault.　●
5　No problem.　●　　　　　　●　謝られたとき
6　Please forgive me.　●

音声のポイント　　つながる音 (1)　

子音で終わる単語の後に母音で始まる単語が続くと、2つの語がつながって聞こえることがあります。このような現象は「連結」や「linking」と呼ばれます。

以下の文の発音を聞いて、下線でつながっている音と音がつながって聞こえることを意識しながら、声に出して発音練習をしよう。

1　I cannot log_into the university system.
2　Enter your username_and password here.
3　Can you fill_it_in, please?
4　I'm_afraid they don't have_it_available_in_English.
5　I can translate_it_into English for you.

59

READING

Oops! Forgot your password?

Visit ICT Office.

or

Access the QR code here.

Please note that it costs 500 yen to issue your new password.

1 Warm-up for Reading

イラストを見ながら 1-3 の音声を聞き、内容が合っていれば T、合っていなければ F を選ぼう。

1 You see this notice when you enter the correct password.　　T / F

2 You need to pay for your new password.　　T / F

3 You can use the QR code to fix the problem.　　T / F

2 Words and Phrases (2)

1-5 の表現の意味に最も近いものを a-e から選ぼう。

1　access　　　　　　　　a　～をリセットする

2　issue　　　　　　　　　b　～を前もって設定する

3　preset　　　　　　　　c　安全

4　security　　　　　　　d　入手する、近づく

5　reset　　　　　　　　　e　発行する

UNIT 7   I've forgotten my password.

 **Reading**

以下の注意書きを読んで、1-3 の答えとして最もふさわしいものを選ぼう。

Your ID and PASSWORD for logging into the university system.

Login ID: **qw23456**
Preset password: **qw23456**

- Change the password when you log in for the first time.
- Remember your password. You will need it every time you use the computers on campus.
- For your security, never share your password with anyone.
- Do not forget to log out when you leave the computer room. Before logging out, save all the necessary files in your personal folder. They will be deleted when you log out.
- To reset your password, you will need your name, date of birth, and email address.

---

1 What should students NOT do?
   A Change passwords.   B Use the computers on campus.
   C Share passwords with friends.   D Log off before leaving the room.

2 Why is it necessary to keep the files in the personal folder?
   A Because you may forget to log off.
   B Because the files won't be kept in the computer.
   C Because you may forget your password.
   D Because the password was preset.

3 What do you need to get a new password?
   A Your login ID.   B Your initial password.
   C Your credit card number.   D Your birthday.

61

4 Share Your Opinions 2-14, 15

a Unit 7 では、パスワードを忘れて迷惑をかけた場面で、謝る表現を学びました。以下の質問に対するあなたの答えを、ヒントを参考にしながらまとめよう。

1 Have you ever experienced difficulties with your computer?
   Your answer:

   _____
   _____

> **Hint**
> - Yes, it …
>   can be very slow.
>   often freezes.
>   was infected by a virus.
> - No, I …
>   have good luck with my computer.
>   have always been good at IT.
>   can make my own repairs.

2 You did something wrong and made your friend feel bad.
   Question: How do you apologize?
   Your answer:

   _____
   _____

> **Hint**
> - I'm sorry for _____. It won't happen again, I promise.
> - I did _____, and it's my fault.
> - Please forgive me. I have learned my lesson from _____.

b 上の質問に対するクラスメイトの答えを、以下の表にまとめよう。

Name	a 1	a 2

UNIT 7　I've forgotten my password.

5　Grammar Practice: 前置詞・接続詞　 2-16, 17

前置詞とは名詞、もしくは名詞のかたまり（名詞句）の前に置かれる語です。日本語では「机の下に」のように名詞（机）の後に「〜の下に」が置かれます。英語では 'under the desk' となり、語順が異なりますので注意しましょう。前置詞と混乱しやすいのが接続詞です。接続詞は文と文をつなぐ役割をします。

前置詞	接続詞
during / because of / despite of / instead of	while / because / although / though
Don't use the smartphone <u>during the meeting</u>.	Don't use the smartphone <u>while you are in the meeting</u>.

a 音声を聞き、以下の文の空欄を埋めよう。

1　_____ your security, never share your password with anyone.

2　I can't do that _____ I've forgotten my password.

3　They will be deleted _____ you log out.

b 音声を聞き、次の語句を並び替えて文を完成させよう。（文頭の文字は大文字に変えよう。）

1　その部屋にはテーブルが一つあります。
　[a table / in / is / the room / there].

2　ログアウトする時には個人情報を消しましょう。
　[delete / personal information / when / you log out / your].

3　パソコンの代わりにタブレットも使用できます。
　[a computer / a tablet / also use / instead of / you can].

63

UNIT 8 I see what you mean.

気持ちはわかるよ

🎧 LISTENING

Students are spending time in the counseling center.

🎧 1 Warm-up for Listening

イラストを見ながら 1-3 の音声を聞き、内容が合っていれば T、合っていなければ F を選ぼう。

1	They are listening to a lecture.	T / F
2	Some students are sitting on the sofa.	T / F
3	Two students are looking at the same computer screen.	T / F

🎧 2 Words and Phrases (1)

1-5 の表現の意味に最も近いものを a-e から選ぼう。

1	counseling center	a	〜をともめる、〜に困る
2	have trouble with	b	カウンセリングセンター
3	consult	c	似たような
4	similar	d	相談する
5	directly	e	直接に

UNIT 8   I see what you mean.

🎧 3   Listening Comprehension   2-20~24

イヴァン（留学生）とマリの会話を聞いて、1-5の質問に対する正しい答えを選ぼう。

1 Where did Ivan find the card?
   ❏ He found it in the bathroom.
   ❏ He found it in the counseling center.

2 What can Ivan do in the counseling center?
   ❏ He can talk about his problems.
   ❏ He can talk about Mari's problems.

3 Does Ivan think his professor is helpful?
   ❏ Yes, he does.
   ❏ No, he doesn't.

4 Has Mari ever had trouble with her teacher?
   ❏ Yes, she has.
   ❏ No, she hasn't.

5 Did Mari talk to her teacher about her problem?
   ❏ Yes, she did.
   ❏ No, she didn't.

 **Dictation**

イヴァンとマリの会話をもう一度聞き、空欄を埋めよう。

1. Ivan: Mari, I _____ this _____ in the _____ upstairs.
   Mari: Oh, it's about the counseling center.
   Ivan: Can you tell me more about it?

2. Mari: You can _____ with the staff about your _____.
   Ivan: So there is somebody to listen to me.
   Mari: You're right. Is there anything you want to talk about?

3. Ivan: I have some trouble with my professor.
   Mari: I'm sorry to hear that. What happened?
   Ivan: I feel like he _____ _____ to _____ me with my research.

4. Mari: I know how you feel.
   Ivan: Have you had a _____ _____?
   Mari: _____. My professor is nice, but she doesn't talk much. So I felt she wasn't helping me enough.

5. Ivan: How did you solve the problem?
   Mari: Well, I _____ to her _____ about it. She understood my feelings.
   Ivan: Oh, that's good.

UNIT 8　I see what you mean.

🎧 5　Useful Expressions: Agreements

マリは "I know how you feel." という表現を使って、イヴァンの気持ちに理解を示しました。こういった場面では、以下のような表現も役立ちます。どんなときに使える表現なのか考えて線でつなごう。

1　I agree with you.　　●
2　I know why you feel that way.　　●　　●　理解を示すとき
3　I'm not so sure about that.　　●
4　Sorry, but I don't think so.　　●
5　That's not always true.　　●　　●　意見に同意できないとき
6　Yes, you are right.　　●

音声のポイント　　つながる音 (2)

子音で終わる単語の後に「ヤ・ユ・ヨ」に似た音で始まる単語が続くときや、"r" で終わる単語の後に母音で始まる単語が続くときにも、2つの語がつながって聞こえることがあります。

以下の文の発音を聞いて、下線でつながっている音と音がつながって聞こえることを意識しながら、声に出して発音練習をしよう。

1　Can_you tell me more_about_it?
2　So there_is somebody to listen to me.
3　Is there_anything you want to talk_about?
4　Have_you had_a similar_experience?
5　My professor_is nice.

67

READING

Are you in trouble?
Do you feel depressed?
You have nobody to talk to?
LET US KNOW.
Student Counseling Center
Location: 1st floor, Building F
Open hours: 10:00-16:00, Monday-Friday
Find us on WhereApp: We_Are_Here_To_Help_You

1 Warm-up for Reading

イラストを見ながら 1-3 の音声を聞き、内容が合っていれば T、合っていなければ F を選ぼう。

1	This message is for students who need help.	T / F
2	It shows where the counseling center is.	T / F
3	You can visit there on weekends.	T / F

2 Words and Phrases (2)

1-5 の表現の意味に最も近いものを a-e から選ぼう。

1	care about		a	〜と連絡をとる
2	contact		b	〜を気にかける
3	appointment		c	人目につかない
4	private		d	仲間、同僚
5	peer		e	予約、約束

68

UNIT 8   I see what you mean.

3 Reading

以下の案内を読んで、1-3の答えとして最もふさわしいものを選ぼう。

Student Counseling Center
College life can sometimes be hard. We are here to help because we care about you.

✧ **Counselors' office**
Contact us about any problem you have. You can make an appointment online, or visit us directly. You can find the office on your left after entering building F.

✧ **Private counseling room**
You can talk to a counselor about any worries you may have. If you don't want to meet your friends in the building, let us know in advance. We will leave the door unlocked so you can enter the private room directly from outside.

✧ **Peer support room**
It's the largest room in building F. Meet our trained peer supporters who can help you.

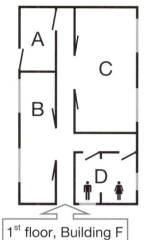

1st floor, Building F

1 Which one is the counselors' office?
   A Room A.   B Room B.   C Room C.   D Room D.

2 What is one of the features of the private counseling room?
   A You can talk to your friends.   B It has direct access from outside.
   C It has trained peer supporters.   D You can leave the room anytime.

3 Which one is the peer support room?
   A Room A.   B Room B.   C Room C.   D Room D.

4 Share Your Opinions

 2-30, 31

a Unit 8 では、友人が困ったことに遭遇している場面で、理解を示す表現を学びました。以下の質問に対するあなたの答えを、ヒントを参考にしながらまとめよう。

1 Have you ever had trouble communicating with your teachers?
Your answer:
_____
_____

Hint

- Yes, I sometimes…
    feel uneasy talking with them.
    have difficulty understanding them.
    miss a chance to meet them.

- No, I…
    listen to them carefully.
    can ask when I don't understand.
    am good at communication.

2 Your friend is in trouble with the boss at his/her part-time job.
Question: How do you show understanding of her/his feelings?
Your answer:
_____
_____

Hint

- You are right. I'm here whenever you want me to _____.
- I agree with you. I think you should talk to _____.
- I know why you feel that way. I had a similar experience when _____.

b 上の質問に対するクラスメイトの答えを、以下の表にまとめよう。

Name	a 1	a 2

UNIT 8   I see what you mean.

5 Grammar Practice: 形容詞   2-32, 33

名詞を修飾するのが形容詞です。名詞の前に置いて名詞の性質や形態を表現します。例えば、girl の前に tall を置くと背の高い女の子となります。形容詞の置く位置は日本語と同じで基本的には名詞の前です。形容詞は名詞の前において、その名詞を修飾する以外に、主語の位置にある名詞の説明をします。例えば That girl is tall. のような場合です。名詞を修飾するには現在分詞や過去分詞も利用します。A sleeping girl のような表現です。形容詞は名詞の前でしたが、現在・過去分詞の場合、一語の場合は名詞の前、2 語以上の場合は名詞の後に置かれます。

a 音声を聞き、以下の文の空欄を埋めよう。

1 My professor is _____.

2 You can enter the _____ room directly from outside.

3 Meet our _____ peer supporters who can help you.

b 音声を聞き、次の語句を並び替えて文を完成させよう。（文頭の文字は大文字に変えよう。）

1 自分の悩みごとの話をするのは難しい。
　[about / difficult / it is / my problems / to talk].

2 深刻な問題があれば電話をしてください。
　[call us / have / if / serious problems / you].

3 私の隣に座っている男の子はロシア出身です。
　[from Russia / is / next to me / sitting / the boy].

UNIT 9 Good job!
よくがんばったね

LISTENING

Sofia and Ken are working at a nursing home.

🎧 1 Warm-up for Listening

イラストを見ながら 1-3 の音声を聞き、内容が合っていれば T、合っていなければ F を選ぼう。

1 They are in a dining room.　　　　　　　　　　　　　　T / F
2 All of them are sitting in wheelchairs.　　　　　　　　　T / F
3 They are preparing their lunch together.　　　　　　　　T / F

🎧 2 Words and Phrases (1)

1-5 の表現の意味に最も近いものを a-e から選ぼう。

1	nursing home	a	〜に参加する
2	participate in	b	コツ
3	memorize	c	覚える
4	encourage	d	励ます
5	tip	e	老人ホーム

UNIT 9   Good job!

3 | Listening Comprehension   2-36~40

ソフィア（留学生）とケンの会話を聞いて、1-5 の質問に対する正しい答えを選ぼう。

1 Where is Sofia going this month?
   ❑ She is visiting a nursing home.
   ❑ She is visiting Ken's home.

2 What does Ken's grandmother do?
   ❑ She participates in the training.
   ❑ She stays in a nursing home.

3 Can Sofia meet Ken's grandmother in the training?
   ❑ Yes, she can.
   ❑ No, she can't.

4 Does Ken try to memorize people's names?
   ❑ Yes, he does.
   ❑ No, he doesn't.

5 Does Ken encourage Sofia to treat the residents as children?
   ❑ Yes, he does.
   ❑ No, he doesn't.

73

 **Dictation**

ソフィアとケンの会話をもう一度聞き、空欄を埋めよう。

1. Sofia: I'm going to _____ a _____ _____ this month.
   Ken: As a volunteer? I'm so proud of you!
   Sofia: Thanks. I need the training for my teacher's license.

2. Ken: Is it your first time visiting a nursing home?
   Sofia: Yes. Have you participated in the training before?
   Ken: No, but my _____ _____ in a _____ _____.

3. Sofia: Then, _____ I _____ her there?
   Ken: _____. She's at a different home.
   Sofia: I see. Are there any tips on how to behave during the training?

4. Ken: I always call my grandma's friends by their names.
   Sofia: Nice. It's a good way to communicate with anyone.
   Ken: I know. So, I _____ to _____ their _____.

5. Sofia: Should I say something nice to encourage them?
   Ken: Yes, but _____ _____ them as _____.
   Sofia: Thanks, Ken. I really appreciate your advice.

5 Useful Expressions: Compliments

ケンは "I'm so proud of you!" という表現を使って、ソフィアの計画を褒めました。こういった場面では、以下のような表現も役立ちます。どんなときに使える表現なのか考えて線でつなごう。

1 Good for you.
2 I appreciate that.
3 I really like….
4 It's nice of you to say that.
5 Thank you so much!
6 That's awesome!

● 褒めるとき

● 褒められたとき

音声のポイント　聞こえなくなる音 (1)

/p, t, k, b, d, g/ のような「破裂音」は、後ろに子音が続くときや、文の切れ目の最後にあるとき、聞こえにくくなることがあります。このような現象は「脱落」や「dropping」と呼ばれます。

以下の文の発音を聞いて、(カッコ) で示した音が聞こえにくくなっていることを意識しながら、声に出して発音練習をしよう。

1 I nee(d) the training for my teacher's license.
2 Is it your firs(t) time visiting a nursing home?
3 She's at a differen(t) home.
4 It's a goo(d) way to communica(te) with anyone.
5 Yes, but avoi(d) treating them as children.

READING

Sunflower Nursing Home Staff Training

Watch out for these words when talking to residents.

Well done.   Good job!   Excellent!

By using these phrases, you are judging the residents.
Remember, you are **NOT** their teacher or their parent.

 Warm-up for Reading

イラストを見ながら 1-3 の音声を聞き、内容が合っていれば T、合っていなければ F を選ぼう。

1 You should use these words with nursing home residents.   T / F
2 You should avoid judging the residents.   T / F
3 You have to act like a teacher.   T / F

 Words and Phrases (2)

1-5 の表現の意味に最も近いものを a-e から選ぼう。

1 resident   a さもなければ
2 technique   b 技術、テクニック
3 considerate   c 居住者
4 characteristics   d 思いやりのある
5 otherwise   e 特徴、特性

UNIT 9 Good job!

3 Reading

以下のパンフレットを読んで、1-3 の答えとして最もふさわしいものを選ぼう。

Communication Techniques in Nursing Homes

❀ **Watch your manners.**
Some residents cannot walk easily as you do. But it does not mean they went back to being babies. Be polite.

❀ **Be considerate.**
Different residents have different characteristics. Try to understand them. Otherwise, they won't understand you. Help them feel comfortable receiving care.

❀ **Speak slowly and clearly.**
Some residents have hearing difficulties, but do not shout. Just speak slowly and clearly.

---

1 What is emphasized in this brochure?
   A Communication skills.   B Knowledge of housing.
   C Knowledge about babies.   D Parenting skills.

2 It is necessary to understand the characteristics of each _____.
   A baby   B home
   C nurse   D resident

3 Which one is encouraged as an appropriate technique?
   A Walk as fast as you can.   B Treat residents as babies.
   C Keep a pleasant atmosphere.   D Shout as loudly as possble.

77

4 Share Your Opinions 2-46, 47

a Unit 9 では、初対面の人と接する場面でコミュニケーションを円滑にする方法を学びました。以下の質問に対するあなたの答えを、ヒントを参考にしながらまとめよう。

1 Are you good at memorizing people's names?
   Your answer:
   _____
   _____

> **Hint**
> - Yes. I try to remember names by…
>   repeating them.
>   writing them down.
>   connecting them with something.
> - No, especially when…
>   I'm tired.
>   there are many people.
>   their names sound unfamiliar.

2 Your friend helped a person in a wheel chair.
   Question: How do you express your feelings?
   Your answer:
   _____
   _____

> **Hint**
> - Good for you. You are always _____ .
> - I really like _____ . Do you always do it?
> - I heard that you _____ . That's awesome!

b 上の質問に対するクラスメイトの答えを、以下の表にまとめよう。

Name	a 1	a 2

UNIT 9　Good job!

📖5　Grammar Practice: 副詞　 2-48, 49

文全体や句などを修飾するのが副詞です。動詞や文の状態や程度を詳しく描写するために用います。副詞の置く位置は文の意味によってさまざまです。頻度を表す副詞の場合、一般動詞であればその前に、be動詞であればその後に置くことが多いです。その他の副詞の場合、表現したい意味によって置く場所が異なることも多くあります。さまざまな文に触れ学習していきましょう。

a 音声を聞き、以下の文の空欄を埋めよう。

1　I _____ call my grandma's friends by their names.

2　Some residents cannot walk _____ as you do.

3　Speak _____ and _____ .

b 音声を聞き、次の語句を並び替えて文を完成させよう。（文頭の文字は大文字に変えよう。）

1　外は寒いので温かい服を着なさい。
　[cold outside / dress / is / it / warmly because].

2　バスに乗るために速く走らなければなりませんでした。
　[fast / I had to / run / the bus / to catch].

3　大体いつも何時に晩御飯を食べますか？
　[do / have dinner / usually / what time / you]?

79

UNIT 10 Come and join us!
一緒にやってみない？

🎧 LISTENING

People are running in a marathon event.

🎧 1 Warm-up for Listening   2-50

イラストを見ながら 1-3 の音声を聞き、内容が合っていれば T、合っていなければ F を選ぼう。

1	It is raining heavily.	T / F
2	Everyone is wearing the same hat.	T / F
3	One of the runners is getting a drink.	T / F

🎧 2 Words and Phrases (1)   2-51

1-5 の表現の意味に最も近いものを a-e から選ぼう。

1	marathon	a	〜を説得する
2	sign up	b	マラソン
3	decline	c	行われる
4	be held	d	参加する、入会手続きをする
5	convince	e	断る、拒否する

80

UNIT 10 Come and join us!

🎧 3 Listening Comprehension   2-52~56

エリック（留学生）とマリの会話を聞いて、1-5 の質問に対する正しい答えを選ぼう。

1 Is Mari inviting Eric to run a marathon race?
   ❏ Yes, she is.
   ❏ No, she isn't.

2 What does Mari need to do to join the team?
   ❏ She needs to sign up.
   ❏ She needs to buy a ticket.

3 Does Mari have to stay outside?
   ❏ Yes, she does.
   ❏ No, she doesn't.

4 What is Mari good at?
   ❏ She is good at working inside the building.
   ❏ She is good at encouraging people.

5 Does Mari want to decline the invitation now?
   ❏ Yes, she does.
   ❏ No, she doesn't.

 **Dictation**

エリックとマリの会話をもう一度聞き、空欄を埋めよう。

1. Eric: Mari, will you _____ us as a _____ _____ _____?
   Mari: Maybe. What kind of event is it?
   Eric: It's for the ABC Marathon which will be held next month.

2. Mari: Thanks for asking me. It sounds like a lot of fun.
   Eric: Yes, _____ _____ to _____ our _____ _____.
   Mari: Wait, Eric. Do I need to stay outside all day long?

3. Eric: You _____ _____ to be _____ at all.
   Mari: Then, what do I do?
   Eric: We need someone who welcomes runners before the race.

4. Mari: You mean that I only work inside the building?
   Eric: Yes, you are the best person for the job.
   Mari: Well, I'm quite _____ at _____ _____ _____.

5. Eric: Now, you have _____ _____ to _____, Mari.
   Mari: You're good at convincing me. Now I _____ to _____.
   Eric: Fantastic. Please come to the staff meeting this afternoon.

82

UNIT 10 Come and join us!

🎧 5 Useful Expressions: Invitations

エリックは "Will you join us as a volunteer staff member?" という表現を使って、マリをボランティア活動に誘いました。こういった場面では、以下のような表現も役立ちます。どんなときに使える表現なのか考えて線でつなごう。

1 Do you want to…?　　　●
2 I was wondering if….　●　　　　　●誘うとき
3 I'd be happy to….　　　●
4 Sorry, I can't because….●
5 That sounds exciting!　●　　　　　●誘われたとき
6 Why don't we…?　　　●

音声のポイント　　聞こえなくなる音 (2)

同じ子音や似た子音が前後に続くときにも、子音が聞こえにくくなることがあります。音がすっかりなくなるわけではなく、脱落した部分に一瞬の空白ができます。

以下の文の発音を聞いて、(カッコ)で示した音が聞こえにくくなっていることを意識しながら、声に出して発音練習をしよう。

1 Wha(t) kind of event is it?
2 It sounds like a lot o(f) fun.
3 Then, wha(t) do I do?
4 Yes, you are the bes(t) person for the job.
5 Come to the sta(ff) meeting this afternoon.

83

READING

ABC Marathon Volunteer Organization Chart

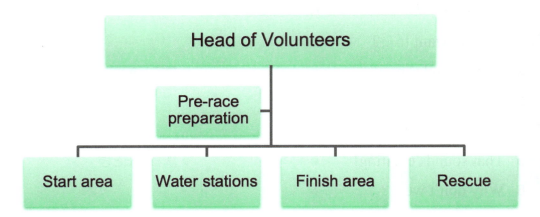

1 Warm-up for Reading

イラストを見ながら 1-3 の音声を聞き、内容が合っていれば T、合っていなければ F を選ぼう。

1 This chart shows the different kinds of volunteer roles.　　T / F

2 Some volunteer members work before the race day.　　T / F

3 Runners can get water at the train station.　　T / F

2 Words and Phrases (2)

1-5 の表現の意味に最も近いものを a-e から選ぼう。

1 policy　　　　　　　　　a 〜の場合に

2 postpone　　　　　　　b 〜を延期する

3 in the case of　　　　　c ポリシー、方針

4 organizer　　　　　　　d 主催者

5 offer　　　　　　　　　e 申し出、提案

UNIT 10 Come and join us!

 **Reading** 2-61

以下の web チャット記録を読んで、1-3 の答えとして最もふさわしいものを選ぼう。

19:20	VOLUNTEER WANTED! The ABC Marathon will be held in Kobe next January. Click here for more info.
19:24	Hi there. Do you have a policy for postponing the event in the case of bad weather? I am available only on the second Sunday in January.
19:30	Dear organizer: Thanks for the invitation. I have just signed up as a registration desk staff. Dear volunteer members: If you are worried about your Japanese language skills, let me know. I can help you in English.
19:31	>To : Thanks for your offer. I wasn't sure if I should sign up because of my bad Japanese, but I will join you. Find Peter on the volunteer list. Looking forward to seeing you!
19:32	I worked as a water server last year. It was a wonderful experience to be part of the team. I want to invite everyone to sign up. Let's make it an event that everyone can enjoy together.

1 You can find details of the event by _____ .
   A going to Kobe   B clicking "Click here"
   C postponing the event   D thanking the organizer

2 Who is Peter?
   A A volunteer staff member.   B A marathon runner.
   C A Japanese native speaker. D An organizer of the event.

3 What is the main purpose of the message posted at 19:32?
   A Complaint.   B Apology.
   C Invitation. D Refusal.

85

4 Share Your Opinions

 2-62, 63

a Unit 10 では、ボランティア活動を始める場面で、友達を誘う表現を学びました。以下の質問に対するあなたの答えを、ヒントを参考にしながらまとめよう。

1. Are you interested in working as a volunteer?
   Your answer:
   _____
   _____

> **Hint**
>
> • Yes, because…
>   I've worked as a volunteer before.
>   I'd like to help others.
>   I'll try it when I have a chance.
>
> • No, because…
>   I'm a bit shy to meet new people.
>   I have other things to do.
>   I want to get paid for what I do.

2. You need to invite some members to your group.
   Question: How do you ask your friends to join the group?
   Your answer:
   _____
   _____

> **Hint**
>
> • Do you have some time now? I was wondering if _____ .
> • Can I talk to you now? I belong to _____ . Do you want to join us?
> • Hi, I'm in _____ . Why don't we do it together?

b 上の質問に対するクラスメイトの答えを、以下の表にまとめよう。

Name	a 1	a 2

UNIT 10 Come and join us!

5 | Grammar Practice: 関係代名詞   2-64, 65

関係代名詞は名詞の後に置かれ、その名詞を修飾します。大きな塊の形容詞のようなものです。修飾される名詞（先行詞と呼ばれます）の種類や、文の中での位置によって使用する関係代名詞が異なります。また、関係代名詞の中でも that は人でも人以外でもどちらにも使用可能です。

先行詞	主格	所有格	目的格
人	who	whose	whom
人以外	which	whose	which

a 音声を聞き、以下の文の空欄を埋めよう。

1 It's for the ABC Marathon _____ will be held next month.

2 We need someone _____ welcomes runners before the race.

3 Let's make it an event _____ everyone can enjoy together.

b 音声を聞き、次の語句を並び替えて文を完成させよう。（文頭の文字は大文字に変えよう。）

1 ボランティアをしたい学生は申し込みしなくてはならない。
[are willing to / must sign up / students / volunteer / who].

2 お互いのことを知り合うためのパーティーをしよう。
[each other / get to know / let's have a party / we can / where].

3 来週に実施されるミーティングに出席すべきでしょうか？
[attend the meeting / next week / should I / which / will be held]?

87

UNIT 11 This will definitely help you.

就活必勝法

🎧 LISTENING

Sara is asking Ken how to write her resume.

🎧 1 Warm-up for Listening

イラストを見ながら1-3の音声を聞き、内容が合っていればT、合っていなければFを選ぼう。

1 Two students are in a photo studio.　　　　　　　　　　T / F
2 They seem to have different opinions.　　　　　　　　　T / F
3 They are taking pictures together.　　　　　　　　　　T / F

🎧 2 Words and Phrases (1)

1-5の表現の意味に最も近いものをa-eから選ぼう。

1 definitely   a 〜を確かめる
2 suitable   b 就職活動
3 job hunting   c 〜を信頼する
4 make sure   d 絶対に
5 trust   e 適切な

UNIT 11　This will definitely help you.

🎧 3　Listening Comprehension

サラ（留学生）とケンの会話を聞いて、1-5 の質問に対する正しい答えを選ぼう。

1　Is Sara writing her resume in English?
　❏ Yes, she is.
　❏ No, she isn't.

2　Is Sara good at taking selfies?
　❏ Yes, she is.
　❏ No, she isn't.

3　Why are the photos taken in photo studios better?
　❏ Because they are more suitable.
　❏ Because they are more expensive.

4　Does Ken tell Sara to wear a formal suit?
　❏ Yes, he does.
　❏ No, he doesn't.

5　Which studio does Ken recommend?
　❏ The one on campus.
　❏ The one in town.

 **Dictation**

サラとケンの会話をもう一度聞き、空欄を埋めよう。

1. Sara: Hey Ken, I need your help with my resume.
   Ken: You're trying to write a _____-_____ _____, right?
   Sara: _____, and it says that I need to paste my photo.

2. Ken: If it's for job hunting, you should take a good photo.
   Sara: All right. I'm _____ at _____ _____.
   Ken: No, Sara, you shouldn't use your selfies.

3. Sara: Why not?
   Ken: The ones _____ in _____ _____ are _____ _____ than selfies.
   Sara: Well, I guess you're right.

4. Ken: Also, _____ _____ to _____ a _____ _____.
   Sara: OK. Any place you recommend for good photos?
   Ken: I believe the one on campus is the best.

5. Sara: Is the _____ on _____ _____ than the studio in town?
   Ken: _____, because it's less expensive.
   Sara: I see. I trust you, Ken.

UNIT 11 This will definitely help you.

Useful Expressions: Persuasion 2-73

ケンは "You should take a good photo." という表現を使って、サラに証明写真を撮るように促しました。こういった場面では、以下のような表現も役立ちます。どんなときに使える表現なのか考えて線でつなごう。

1 I don't think so.　　　　　　　●
2 I'm sure you could….　　　　●　　　● 相手に行動を促すとき
3 I'm telling you to… because….　●
4 Listen. You definitely need….　●
5 OK, I'll do it.　　　　　　　　●　　　● 行動を促されたとき
6 Right. I'd be happy to….　　　●

音声のポイント　　まじりあう音 (1)　 2-74

/t/ や /d/ で終わる単語の後に「ヤ・ユ・ヨ」に似た音で始まる単語が続くとき、単語の境目の音が別の音に変化することがあります。このような現象は「同化」や「assimilation」と呼ばれます。

以下の文の発音を聞いて、[角カッコ] で示した音が変化していることを意識しながら、声に出して発音練習をしよう。

1 I nee[d y]our help with my resume.
2 You shouldn't u[se y]our selfies.
3 Well, I gue[ss y]ou're right.
4 Any pla[ce y]ou recommend for good photos?
5 I trus[t y]ou, Ken.

91

READING

SARA AYAD
Environmental Science Researcher

contact:
+81-80-1234-5678

EDUCATION
University of XYZ
2025-2029
Bachelor of Sciences, Environmental Science

1 Warm-up for Reading 2-75

イラストを見ながら 1-3 の音声を聞き、内容が合っていれば T、合っていなければ F を選ぼう。

1	This is part of Sara's resume.	T / F
2	This is a common resume in Japan.	T / F
3	Sara has experience in scientific research.	T / F

2 Words and Phrases (2) 2-76

1-5 の表現の意味に最も近いものを a-e から選ぼう。

1	career development	a	〜を登録する
2	register	b	〜を描写する、説明する
3	consider	c	キャリア開発
4	describe	d	考慮する
5	qualification	e	素質、資格

UNIT 11 This will definitely help you.

 Reading   2-77

以下の指示を読んで、1-3 の答えとして最もふさわしいものを選ぼう。

Job Hunting — Ready, Set, Go!

What do you need to do for job hunting? To focus on your career development, follow these steps:

#1. **Get ready.** Take your time doing research. You definitely need to study what kinds of jobs are out there. Sign up to receive job information. Register yourself to the networking websites. Information is the key to success.

#2. **Get set.** Consider how you would like to describe yourself to your employers. Then you will realize what experience and qualifications you need to have. It's never too late to start improving your qualifications.

#3. **Go!** Practice makes perfect. Apply for as many job interviews as possible. Talking with recruiters is the best way to get used to the situation. You may also ask your friends and family to play the role of the recruiters.

Now, take your first step as soon as possible!

1 This list is for those who are looking for _____ .
   A a job   B a worker
   C a webpage developer   D a researcher

2 Which of the following is NOT on this list?
   A To check the networking sites.   B To improve your skills.
   C To copy your friends' resumes.   D To rehearse job interviews.

3 The first thing you should do is gather _____ .
   A information   B house keys   C employees   D family

93

4 Share Your Opinions

 2-78, 79

a Unit 11 では、就職活動の場面で、履歴書の書き方を説く方法を学びました。以下の質問に対するあなたの答えを、ヒントを参考にしながらまとめよう。

1 Have you ever applied for a part-time job?
   Your answer:
   _____
   _____

Hint

- Yes, I wanted to…
   have experience working.
   save money for myself.
   work with my friends.

- No, because…
   I want to focus on my studies.
   my parents don't allow me to.
   I don't have time.

2 Your friend is planning to skip an important exam.
   Question: How do you try to change her/his mind?
   Your answer:
   _____
   _____

Hint

- Listen. You definitely need to take the exam because….
- I'm telling you to do your best because….
- I'm sure you could pass the exam if you….

b 上の質問に対するクラスメイトの答えを、以下の表にまとめよう。

Name	a 1	a 2

UNIT 11　This will definitely help you.

5　Grammar Practice: 比較 2-80, 81

あるものが他のものと比較し最も〜だ、のように二つかそれ以上のものを比較する際には形容詞・副詞を変化させます。一般的には2音節以内の形容詞の場合、形容詞の末尾に er/est をつけますが、音節数がそれ以上の場合 more/most を形容詞の前に置きます。

	比較級	最上級
tall	Jane is taller than Jimmy.	Jane is the tallest in her class.
expensive	This watch is more expensive than that one.	This watch is the most expensive one in that store.

a 音声を聞き、以下の文の空欄を埋めよう。

1　I believe the one on campus is _____ _____.

2　Is the one on campus _____ _____ the studio in town?

3　Apply for ____ _____ job interviews ____ possible.

b 音声を聞き、次の語句を並び替えて文を完成させよう。（文頭の文字は大文字に変えよう。）

1　スタジオで撮った写真は自撮り写真よりはっきりしている。
[are / clearer / taken in the studio / than selfies / the pictures].

2　企業研究は就職活動で最も重要な点である。
[company research / is / job hunting / part of / the most important].

3　どちらの店の方が学校に近いですか？
[closer to / is / our school / shop / which]?

95

UNIT 12 Thanks for everything.

今までありがとう

🎧 LISTENING

Julius and Mari are at the airport.

🎧 1 Warm-up for Listening 2-82

イラストを見ながら 1-3 の音声を聞き、内容が合っていれば T、合っていなければ F を選ぼう。

1 They are on the airplane. — T / F
2 One student is giving a letter to the other. — T / F
3 They both seem to be very happy. — T / F

🎧 2 Words and Phrases (1) 2-83

1-5 の表現の意味に最も近いものを a-e から選ぼう。

1 plenty of...   a （人）に思い出させる
2 boarding   b たくさんの、十分な
3 remind   c 喜び、楽しみ
4 absolutely   d 絶対に
5 pleasure   e 搭乗、乗船

UNIT 12　Thanks for everything.

🎧 3　Listening Comprehension

ジュリアス（留学生）とマリの会話を聞いて、1-5 の質問に対する正しい答えを選ぼう。

1 Who is leaving Japan?
   ❏ Mari is.
   ❏ Julius is.

2 Does Mari give Julius a school mug?
   ❏ Yes, she does.
   ❏ No, she doesn't.

3 Does Julius think that the mug is too heavy?
   ❏ Yes, he does.
   ❏ No, he doesn't.

4 How long did Julius stay in Japan?
   ❏ He stayed in Japan for one year.
   ❏ They didn't mention it.

5 Does Julius want Mari to read the letter now?
   ❏ Yes, he does.
   ❏ No, he doesn't.

97

 **Dictation**

ジュリアスとマリの会話をもう一度聞き、空欄を埋めよう。

1. Julius: Thanks for giving me a ride, Mari.
   Mari: No problem. You have plenty of time before boarding.
   Julius: Right, but I can't believe this is _____ _____ _____ in _____.

2. Mari: Here is a _____ _____ for you.
   Julius: Oh, a _____ _____? That's so kind of you.
   Mari: I hope this will remind you of the times we spent together.

3. Julius: Absolutely, I really appreciate it, Mari.
   Mari: It won't be too heavy if you put it in your suitcase, right?
   Julius: It's _____ _____ ___ ____, so I will carry it.

4. Mari: I wish you could stay in Japan for a little longer.
   Julius: I know. I would stay for _____ _____ __ _____.
   Mari: Can I visit you next year?

5. Julius: Anytime. By the way, here is a letter for you.
   Mari: Thank you so much, Julius.
   Julius: My pleasure. _____ it _____ you _____ _____.

UNIT 12　Thanks for everything.

🎧 5　Useful Expressions: Gratitude 2-89

ジュリアスは "Thanks for giving me a ride." という表現を使って、マリに感謝の気持ちを伝えました。こういった場面では、以下のような表現も役立ちます。どんなときに使える表現なのか考えて線でつなごう。

1　Don't mention it.　　　●
2　I can't thank you enough.　●　　　　　　● お礼を言うとき
3　I really appreciate it.　　●
4　Not at all.　　　　　　●
5　Thank you so much.　　●　　　　　　● お礼を言われたとき
6　You are welcome.　　　●

音声のポイント　　**まじりあう音 (2)**　 2-90

/t/ の音が、強く発音される母音と弱く発音される母音の間にあるとき、特にアメリカ英語では /t/ が別の音に聞こえることがあります。この同化の現象は、単語と単語の間でも、単語の中でも起こる可能性があります。

以下の文の発音を聞いて、[角カッコ] で示した音が変化していることを意識しながら、声に出して発音練習をしよう。

1　You have plen[t]y of time before boarding.
2　Here is a li[tt]le present for you.
3　It won't be too heavy if you pu[t] i[t] in your suitcase, right?
4　I wish you could stay in Japan for a li[tt]le longer.
5　By the way, here is a le[tt]er for you.

READING

The Benefits of Sending a Letter Rather Than an Email

 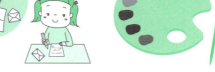 

It's memorable.　　　It's creative.　　　It's heartwarming.

1 Warm-up for Reading 2-91

イラストを見ながら 1-3 の音声を聞き、内容が合っていれば T、合っていなければ F を選ぼう。

1　It shows how to write an email.　　　　　　　　　　T / F
2　Letters tend to remain in people's memories.　　　　T / F
3　Letters give people a warm feeling.　　　　　　　　T / F

2 Words and Phrases (2) 2-92

1-5 の表現の意味に最も近いものを a-e から選ぼう。

1　benefit　　　　　　　a　メリット、利益
2　grateful　　　　　　　b　一生の
3　bright　　　　　　　　c　感謝している
4　lifetime　　　　　　　d　宝物
5　treasure　　　　　　　e　明るい

UNIT 12　Thanks for everything.

3　Reading

以下の手紙を読んで、1-3 の答えとして最もふさわしいものを選ぼう。

Dear Mari,

　Thank you for helping me out every time I had trouble with campus life. You have been one of the most helpful staff members in the student center. Without you, I wouldn't be the student that I am today.
　I would also like to express how grateful I am for your friendship. It always made me happy to see your bright smile and hear your warm words. Getting to know you and spending time with you here in Japan will be a lifetime treasure for me.
　Time flies, and it's time for me to go back to my home country. If you ever have a chance to visit me in Rwanda, I want to take you to my favorite spots. I hope to see you again soon somewhere around the world.
　Thanks again for everything. You meant so much to me.

Best, Thank you!
Julius

1　Who wrote this letter?
　A Mari.　　　　　　　　　B A staff member in the student center.
　C Julius.　　　　　　　　　D Julius's friend in Japan.

2　Where is Julius originally from?
　A Japan.　　　　　　　　　B A student center.
　C Rwanda.　　　　　　　　D Not mentioned.

3　What is Julius trying to tell Mari?
　A Feelings of gratitude.　　B How to fly.
　C Feelings of apology.　　　D How to travel.

101

4 Share Your Opinions

 2-94, 95

a Unit 12 では、お別れの場面で、感謝の気持ちを伝える表現を学びました。以下の質問に対するあなたの答えを、ヒントを参考にしながらまとめよう。

1 Do you often write letters to your friends?
   Your answer:
   _____
   _____

> **Hint**
> - Yes, I prefer writing letters as it's…
>   more personal.
>   more special.
>   more memorable.
> - No, I usually…
>   send text messages.
>   send emails.
>   speak directly to my friends.

2 Your friend helped you when you were in a lot of trouble.
   Question: How do you show your gratitude?
   Your answer:
   _____
   _____

> **Hint**
> - Thank you so much. I'd like to invite you to dinner.
> - I really appreciate it. This is something for you.
> - I can't thank you enough. Let me know whenever you need help.

b 上の質問に対するクラスメイトの答えを、以下の表にまとめよう。

Name	**a** 1	**a** 2

UNIT 12 Thanks for everything.

5 Grammar Practice: 仮定法

 2-96, 97

仮定法とは、実際には起こっていない、現実ではないことを表現する方法です。「私が鳥だったら空を飛べただろうに。」のように実際には鳥ではありませんので、空は飛べません。日本語でも「鳥だったら」「飛べた」のように、現在とは異なる事実を表現するために過去時制を用います。

I wish I were a bird.	もし鳥だったら飛べただろうに。 （鳥ではないから空は飛べない。）
If I had brought an umbrella, I wouldn't have gotten wet.	もし傘を持っていれば濡れずに済んだのに。 （傘を持っていなかったから濡れた。）

a 音声を聞き、以下の文の空欄を埋めよう。

1. I wish you _____ _____ in Japan for a little longer.

2. I _____ _____ for another year __ _ _____.

3. _____ you, I _____ ___ the student that I am today.

b 音声を聞き、次の語句を並び替えて文を完成させよう。（文頭の文字は大文字に変えよう。）

1. 今年の夏あなたが日本に来られたらよいのに。
   [come to / I wish / Japan / this summer / you could].

2. 寝坊しなかったら授業に間に合ったのに。
   [for class / hadn't overslept, / have been on time / I would / if I].

3. もしどの国にでも行けるとしたら、どこに行きますか？
   [any country, / could visit / if you / where / would you go]?

TEXT PRODUCTION STAFF

edited by	編集
Hiroko Nakazawa	中澤 ひろ子

English-language editing by	英文校正
Bill Benfield	ビル・ベンフィールド

cover design by	表紙デザイン
Nobuyoshi Fujino	藤野 伸芳

text design by	本文デザイン
Nobuyoshi Fujino	藤野 伸芳

CD PRODUCTION STAFF

narrated by	吹き込み者
Dominic Allen (American English)	ドミニク・アレン（アメリカ英語）
Howard Colefield (American English)	ハワード・コルフィールド（アメリカ英語）
Karen Haedrich (American English)	カレン・ヘドリック（アメリカ英語）
Rachel Walzer (American English)	レイチェル・ワルザー（アメリカ英語）
Nadia McKechnie (British English)	ナディア・マケックニー（イギリス英語）
Guy Perryman (British English)	ガイ・ペリマン（イギリス英語）
Sarah Greaves (Australian English)	サラ・グリブズ（オーストラリア英語）
et al.	他

Daily English for College Students Book 1
〈場面・機能別〉大学生のための英語 Book1

2025年1月20日　初版発行
2025年2月15日　第2刷発行

編著者　中西 のりこ　平井 愛　Mary Ellis
発行者　佐野 英一郎
発行所　株式会社 成美堂
　　　　〒101-0052 東京都千代田区神田小川町 3-22
　　　　TEL 03-3291-2261　　FAX 03-3293-5490
　　　　http://www.seibido.co.jp

印刷・製本　(株)倉敷印刷

ISBN 978-4-7919-7302-6　　　　　　　　　　　　　Printed in Japan

・落丁・乱丁本はお取り替えします。
・本書の無断複写は、著作権上の例外を除き著作権侵害となります。